FRESH START
FOR
VEGETABLES

*   *

By Julee Rosso
Published by Ivy Books:

FRESH START FOR FRUIT

FRESH START FOR GRAINS & PASTA

FRESH START FOR MEAT & FISH

FRESH START FOR POULTRY

FRESH START FOR SOUP

FRESH START FOR VEGETABLES

FRESH START FOR VEGETABLES

From the bestselling *Fresh Start*

Julee Rosso

Illustrations by Annie Hoffman

IVY BOOKS • NEW YORK

An Ivy Book
Published by The Ballantine Publishing Group
Copyright © 1996 by Julee Rosso Associates, Inc.

http://www.randomhouse.com

Great Good Food is a trademark of Julee Rosso Associates, Inc.

Library of Congress Catalog Card Number: 97-94246

ISBN 0-8041-1706-3

This edition published by arrangement with Crown Publishers, Inc.

Manufactured in the United States of America

First Edition: February 1998

10 9 8 7 6 5 4 3 2 1

* Contents *

v

* Introduction *

* One Step at a Time *

PASTA IS FATTENING. EXERCISE MODERATELY—NO, EXERCISE MORE! EGGS ARE BAD/NOT SO BAD. DRINK WINE! If it's Tuesday, this must be another health proclamation. And somehow, the latest one seems to conflict with the health news we read just last week. No wonder we've become a nation of food skeptics. Admittedly, we're overweight skeptics—with convenience- and junk-food habits, an eye for quantity, and alarming rates of heart disease, cancer, and other ailments linked to lifestyle. But we're skeptics nonetheless. Wearied by the roller-coaster ride of medical and nutritional information, lots of people are throwing up their hands and just eating what they want. *Longevity be damned! Let's eat cheese! Beef is back! Live for today!*

> *"If you have made mistakes . . . there is always another chance for you. You may have a fresh start any moment you choose, for this thing we call 'failure' is not the falling down but the staying down."*
> —MARY PICKFORD

While it would be easier to agree, we must remember that individual studies are only stepping-stones to scientific consensus. We can't overreact to each and every one. We have to rely on established facts and recommendations regarding the relationship between diet and health, such as the Framingham Study, the oldest ongoing research project on cardiovascular disease, which has well-documented results of the positive effect of lower-fat diets on heart disease over the years.

I find America's disease statistics far too disturbing to ignore. For many of us, our lifestyles and family histories are frightening. I am particularly concerned about heart disease, which is now recognized as the leading cause of death for women—just as it is for men. And the American culture of abundance has made us the fattest nation on earth. In this century alone, our average fat intake has risen to 37 percent of our total daily calories, a figure that can quickly spike higher on any given day.

Research repeatedly shows that in cultures around the world where people eat less fat and more carbohydrate-based foods—combined with other lifestyle differences such as exercise and lowered stress—heart disease rates and those for cancer, stroke, and other "modern" diseases are dramatically lower.

Is there a "miracle" diet that we in America don't know about? No, it's simply a diet similar to what our ancestors ate and the one many of the world's populations consume today. It is a diet based on grains, legumes, fruits, and vegetables, with only occasional meat, dairy products, and fat. It is a diet that—because we have so very much abundance in America today—we have forgotten. It is the diet represented in the USDA Food Pyramid.

But all this news doesn't have to be overwhelming or depressing. It just makes it very clear that it's possible to help our health simply by changing how we eat and live today. And once you begin to make these changes, you'll feel better, have more energy, and truly believe that—for the first time ever—*you're* in charge of your own healthful destiny!

✳ It's Your Fresh Start ✳

My goal in writing this cookbook is to make healthful cooking simple and delicious enough to become a daily habit. *Fresh Start for Vegetables* isn't about tricks or gimmicks, synthetic ingredients, magic potions, or food combinations. This is not a weight loss plan, although that may well be a benefit. This book is meant to be a primer for helping you to change your cooking habits and learn to truly enjoy lower-fat foods. It's about fresh, wholesome ingredients and common sense. It's about glorious flavors achieved without the burden of fat. It's about the big, intense tastes I've come to know and love in perfect harmony with today's goal of a healthy, balanced, always-on-the-go lifestyle. And there's only one secret to cooking with less fat—replace it with flavor!

In *Fresh Start for Vegetables*, I don't suggest—even for a minute—that you'll have to sacrifice the pleasure of eating or swap "real foods" for synthetic substitutes. Nor will you have to give up the foods you've come to love. In the recipes that follow I have either adjusted the ingredients or modified the cooking method to lower the fat. Where it is not to my taste to give up the intrinsic flavor of one of my favorite ingredients—such as Parmesan (I use less) or in the cases of whipped cream and coconut—it becomes an indulgence to be enjoyed less frequently. Yet all of the recipes are simple and quick. After cooking them for a while, you will easily know how to adapt most of your own favorites. So let's begin. . . .

✳ What to Eat—and How Much of It to Eat ✳

Restructuring how you eat every day is easy when you visualize the Food Pyramid: Start at the bottom of the pyramid—think of it as building the foundation. Eat more grains and legumes than anything else and don't skimp on fruits and vegetables, either. Go easy on dairy products and meat, poultry, and fish. Work your way up to the point of using fat only to enhance flavors! No more thickly spreading on the butter or pouring on the olive oil! Trust me, after a few weeks of eating this way, you will hardly miss the fat. And when you do eat a high-fat dish, you will find that a little bit goes a long, long way. After several months you will wonder how you ever managed to eat that tremendous slice of cheesecake or plateful of bacon, eggs, and hash browns.

As you consider how to include more grains, legumes, fruits, and vegetables in your diet, remember that the big, bold flavors I have long loved and cooked with shine through in these recipes. They replace the fat, so that you won't miss it for a minute! A squeeze of tangy lemon juice, a sprinkle of sweet balsamic vinegar, a spoonful of aromatic chopped fresh herbs, or a pinch of pungent ground spices enlivens nearly everything. The flavors of the food come alive, dancing on your palate in a pleasingly delicious medley of taste sensations.

> *"The secret of success is consistency of purpose."*
> —BENJAMIN DISRAELI

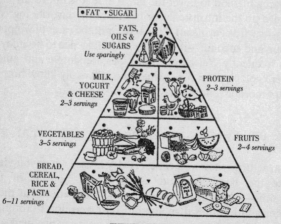

THE USDA FOOD PYRAMID

* Daily Calorie Requirements *

Recommended Energy Intake for You

FIND YOUR AGE, GENDER, AND LIFESTYLE

TYPE OF PERSON AND ACTIVITY LEVEL	CALORIES PER DAY	TYPE OF PERSON AND ACTIVITY LEVEL	CALORIES PER DAY
Minimum calories for adequate nutrition	1,000–1,200	Very active women Average men 50+ Boys 11 to 14	2,200–2,600
Sedentary women	1,600	Active men Teen boys	2,600–2,800
Moderately active women Children 4 to 6 Women 51+	1,800	Men 25 to 50, light to heavy activity Athletes in training	3,000–4,000
Active women Sedentary men Teen girls Children 7 to 10	2,000–2,200		

CONSULT WITH YOUR DOCTOR OR NUTRITIONIST TO CONFIRM YOUR GOAL

SOURCE: U.S. Department of Health, Human Services, Food and Drug Administration, FDA Special Report, May 1993, p. 44, Washington, D.C.

When the Flavor Is There,
* You Forget the Fat Is Gone! *

The biggest secret to cooking with less fat is to replace it with flavor! It's easy for me because my cooking style has always included big, intense, magnified flavors that taste fresh, clear, and clean—and are immediately and easily identifiable.

The most wonderful thing of all is that most of these big, bold flavors come from foods with little, if any, fat. And those that do have a lot (*), such as nuts and olives, have flavors so bold that a little bit goes a long way.

- ◆ **Anchovies***
  - fillets
  - paste
  - rolled with capers
- ◆ **Broths**
  - beef
  - chicken
  - fish
  - vegetable
- ◆ **Capers**
- ◆ **Chilies, fresh, dried, roasted**
  - habañero
  - jalapeño
  - poblano
  - Scotch bonnet
  - serrano
- ◆ **Chili paste**
- ◆ **Chutney**
- ◆ **Citrus juice**
  - grapefruit
  - lemon
  - lime
  - orange
- ◆ **Citrus zest**
  - lemon
  - lime
  - orange
- ◆ **Cocoa powder***
  - alkalized
  - nonalkalized
- ◆ **Coconut, shredded***
- ◆ **Coconut milk***
- ◆ **Coffee and tea**
- ◆ **Dried fruits**
  - apples
  - apricots
  - bananas
  - currants
  - peaches
  - prunes
  - raisins
- ◆ **Fruit and vegetable juices**
  - hand-squeezed
  - store-bought
- ◆ **Fruit-only jams and preserves**
- ◆ **Garlic**
  - fresh
  - puréed
  - roasted
- ◆ **Ginger**
  - crystallized
- fresh
- powdered
- ◆ **Herbs**
  - dried
  - fresh
- ◆ **Honey**
- ◆ **Horseradish**
  - fresh
  - prepared
  - wasabi
- ◆ **Lemongrass**
- ◆ **Mushrooms, fresh and dried**
  - cèpe
  - Chinese black
  - morel
  - porcini
  - shiitake
- ◆ **Mustards**
  - Dijon
  - powdered
  - prepared yellow
  - spicy brown
- ◆ **Nuts***
  - roasted
  - salted
  - toasted
- ◆ **Olives***

- **Peppercorns**
  black
  green
  red
  white
- **Pestos***
- **Prepared sauces**
  hoisin
  hot pepper (such
    as Tabasco)
  Pickapeppa
  soy
  tamari
  Worcestershire
- **Red bell peppers**
  fresh
  grilled

  roasted
- **Salsas**
  homemade
  store-bought
- **Spices**
  dry rubs
  freshly ground in
    a mini food
    processor
  freshly ground
    with a mortar
    and pestle
  spice blends
- **Sun-dried
  tomatoes**
  dry-packed
  oil-packed*

- **Tomato paste**
- **Vanilla**
  beans
  extract
- **Vinegars**
  balsamic
  cider
  herb-infused
  red wine
  rice wine
  white distilled
  white wine
- **Wines**
  fortified
  table

* Fabulous Flavors *

Over the years, I've discovered flavors for foods from all around the world. Some of the flavors have a lot of fat, but many of our favorites have very little fat. Once you know which are which, you'll know how to use them and in what quantities.

	CAL.	FAT (G)		CAL.	FAT (G)
Almonds, 1 T.	38	3	Mushrooms, dried, 1 T.	11	0.04
Anchovies, 1	8	0.4	Mushrooms, fresh, ¼ cup	2	0.03
Balsamic vinegar, 1 T.	2	0	Mustard, 1 T.	11	0.7
Basil, fresh, 1 T.	0.5	0	Nutmeg, 1 T.	37	2
Black olives, 1	12	1	Red pepper, sweet, 1 T.	2.2	0.02
Black pepper, 1 T.	16	0.3	Red pepper flakes, 1 tsp.	11	0.3
Capers, 1 oz.	1	0.1	Red wine, 1 T.	11	0
Caraway seed, 1 T.	7	0.1	Salsa, 1 T.	3	0
Catsup, 1 T.	16	0.1	Spinach pesto, 1 T.	24	1.5
Cinnamon, 1 T.	18	0.2	Sun-dried tomatoes, 1 T.	9	0.1
Coconut, 1 T.	18	1.8	Sun-dried tomatoes,		
Currants, 1 T.	26	0.02	oil-packed, 1 T.	30	2
Garlic, 1 T.	13	0.04	Tabasco, 1 T.	2	0.09
Gingerroot, 1 T.	4	0.04	Tamari, 1 T.	9	0.01
Green olives, 1	7	0.7	Tomato paste, 1 T.	14	0.1
Hoisin sauce, 1 T.	30	0.8	Vanilla, 1 T.	28	0
Horseradish, 1 T.	6	0	White wine, 1 T.	10	0
Lemon juice, 1 T.	4	0.02	Worcestershire sauce, 1 T.	11	0
Lemon zest, 1 T.	6	0.02			

* Vegetable Variety *

VEGETABLES	AMOUNT	CAL.	VIT. A	VIT. C	CALCIUM	FIBER
Alfalfa sprouts	1 cup	10	x	x	x	
Artichoke	1 med	60	x	x	x	
Asparagus	12 med	44	x	x	x	
Beets, cooked	1 cup	52		*		*
Broccoli, cooked	1 cup	24	x	x		*
Brussels sprouts, cooked	1 cup	60	x	x		x
Cabbage, raw	1 cup	18		x		x
Carrot, raw	1 med	31	x	x		x
Cauliflower, cooked	1 cup	25		x		*
Celery, raw	1 stalk	6	x			
Corn, cooked	1 cup	133		x		x
Dandelion greens	1 cup	14	x	x	x	*
Eggplant, cooked	1 cup	26				x
Fennel, raw	1 cup	27		x	x	
Green beans, raw	1 cup	44	*	x		
Green peas, raw	1 cup	117	x	x		x
Green pepper, raw	1 med	28	*	x		
Kale, cooked	1 cup	42	x	x	x	x
Kohlrabi, cooked	1 cup	48		x		
Leek, cooked	1 med	32	x	x	x	x
Lettuce, Boston	1 cup	8	x	*		n/a
Lettuce, iceberg	1 cup	9	x	x		x
Lettuce, leaf	1 cup	10	x	*		
Lettuce, romaine	1 cup	8	x	x		
Mushrooms, raw	1 cup	42		*		*
Mustard greens, cooked	1 cup	28	x	x	x	x
Onions, raw	1 cup	60				*
Parsnips, cooked	1 cup	126		x		x
Potato, baked, with skin	1 med	227	n/a	x		x
Radishes, raw	10 med	7		x		
Red pepper, raw	1 med	28	x	x		
Rutabaga, cooked	1 cup	58		x		*
Snow peas, cooked	1 cup	40		x	x	*
Spinach, raw	1 cup	12	x	x		*

Julee Rosso

VEGETABLES	AMOUNT	CAL.	VIT. A	VIT. C	CALCIUM	FIBER
Summer squash, cooked	1 cup	24	*	*		
Sweet potato, no skin	1 med	206	x	x		x
Swiss chard, cooked	1 cup	36	x	x	x	*
Tomato, raw	1 med	26	*	x		
Turnips, cooked	1 cup	28		x		x
Watercress	1 cup	4	x	x		x
Winter squash, cooked	1 cup	82	x	x		*

x = contains at least 10% of the RDA
* = contains at least 5 to 9% of the RDA
n/a = not available

"*Tomorrow is the most important thing in life. Comes in to us at midnight very clean. It's perfect when it arrives and puts itself in our hands and hopes we've learned something from yesterday.*"

—JOHN WAYNE

✳ Recipes ✳

✳ Blossoming Onion ✳

This deep-fried restaurant favorite really works surprisingly well with an oven-fried method. I'd rather enjoy this more frequently this way than have the onion be such an indulgence. It's great served with Spicy Dipping Sauce (recipe follows).

SERVES 4

2 very large red onions (about 1¹/₂ pounds)
¹/₂ cup plain bread crumbs or Panko (see page 19)
1 teaspoon garlic powder
¹/₂ teaspoon paprika
2 large egg whites

1. Preheat the oven to 375°F. Lightly spray a baking sheet with olive oil spray.
2. Peel the skin from the onions and trim the bottoms so that the onions sit flat. Starting at the center of the top of each onion and working around it, cut 20 to 30 slits, cutting only three-quarters into the onion for a "flower" effect. Transfer to the baking sheet.
3. In a small bowl, combine the bread crumbs, garlic powder, and paprika. Set aside. In another bowl, whisk the egg whites lightly with a fork. Pour the whites over the onions to cover thoroughly and then sprinkle evenly with the seasoned crumbs. Spray lightly with olive oil spray and bake for 40 to 50 minutes, until the onions are lightly browned. Serve immediately.

Cal. 123   Carb. 25g   Prot. 5g   Chol. 0.6mg   Fat 0.9g/5%   Sod. 120mg

11

SPICY DIPPING SAUCE

Spicy and tantalizing, this is reminiscent of the extremely fatty sauce traditionally served with deep-fried blossoming onions—but this version is very low in fat!

MAKES ABOUT 1 CUP

3/4 cup nonfat cottage cheese
1/4 cup mayonnaise
1 1/2 teaspoons prepared horseradish
1 teaspoon cayenne
Salt and freshly ground black pepper to taste

1. In a blender, blend the cottage cheese until smooth.
2. Transfer the cottage cheese to a bowl and add the mayonnaise, horseradish, and cayenne. Season with salt and pepper. Mix well. Store in refrigerator. Bring to room temperature before serving.

Cal. 11   Carb. 0.2g   Prot. 0.5g   Chol. 0.7mg   Fat 0.9g/75%   Sod. 21mg
(analyzed per teaspoon)

PANKO

This is a special Japanese bread crumb coating, fast becoming one of my favorites for oven frying. Pointed crystal-like crumbs stick out in all directions, increasing texture and crispiness even after cooling. Look for it in Asian groceries.

BREAD CRUMBS

You can make your own (and I recommend you do). Process 2- to 3-day-old French bread in a food processor on "pulse" to the desired crumb size. Two ounces of bread yields about 1 cup of fresh crumbs and 1/2 cup of toasted crumbs. For crispy crumbs, toss each cup of crumbs with 1 teaspoon olive oil. Spread on a baking sheet and bake at 325°F for about 12 minutes.

For flavor, add fresh herbs, red pepper flakes, fresh garlic, or cracked black pepper.

* Baby Artichoke Sauté *

While I love whole baby artichokes and often carry them home to Michigan from faraway markets in New York or Italy, I can't do so often enough to satisfy my craving. And so frozen artichokes are called into action. Even these are often not in the market, so stock up when you find them.

SERVES 4

2 teaspoons olive oil
2 tablespoons lemon juice
$^1/_4$ cup low-fat, low-sodium chicken broth
18 ounces frozen artichokes, thawed and halved lengthwise
2 tablespoons finely minced garlic
4 teaspoons finely minced lemon zest
2 ounces turkey ham, sliced paper-thin and minced
$^1/_4$ cup finely minced fresh Italian parsley
Salt and freshly ground black pepper to taste

1. In a large skillet, heat the oil, lemon juice, and chicken broth over medium heat for 1 minute. Add the artichokes, garlic, and lemon zest; cover and cook for 2 to 3 minutes. Uncover, add the ham, and cook, tossing, for 4 to 5 minutes, until the artichokes start to brown.
2. Toss with the parsley and season with salt and pepper. Serve immediately.

Cal. 113   Carb. 17g   Prot. 8g   Chol. 9mg   Fat 3g/21%   Sod. 291mg

THE TASTE OF GREEN

We've noticed that parsley really does make green things taste greener.

We use it daily, tossing in a sprinkle of freshness, a dash of color, and a last-minute sparkle of flavor to a dish. But have you really tasted parsley lately?

There are three kinds available: familiar curly parsley; the more pungent Italian, or flat-leafed, parsley; and Hamburg, rooted, or turnip-rooted parsley, sold in specialty stores only in the late fall and winter. Both the root, which tastes a bit like celeriac, and the leaves of rooted parsley may be used.

And then there's cilantro, sometimes called Chinese parsley because of its appearance, but from an entirely different plant called coriander. Its lacy-looking leaves add fresh-cooked flavor.

Last but best of all is chervil. The color and taste of its tiny lacy leaves evoke the essence of spring. Find a source or grow it yourself.

Never, ever use these dried; after all, it's their freshness that adds the sparkle.

* Baked Potatoes *

A cozy comforting baked potato is one of life's true satisfactions—plus it's full of nutrients and good intentions. As it emerges hot from the oven, think carefully about what you really want to put on top.

	CAL.	FAT (G)/%		
1 medium potato with skin (about 8 ounces)	227	0.3/1		

TOPPINGS (2 TABLESPOONS)	TOPPING ALONE		W/POTATO	
	CAL.	FAT (G)/%	CAL.	FAT (G)/%
Blue cheese	60	5/75	287	5.3/16
Butter	203	23/100	430	23.3/48
Cheddar cheese	57	5/79	284	5.3/16
Chives	2	0/0	229	0.3/1
Cottage cheese, low-fat	21	0.3/11	248	0.6/2
Cottage cheese, nonfat	18	0/0	245	0.3/1
Olive oil	239	27/100	466	27.3/52
Parmesan cheese	57	4/63	284	4.3/13
Salsa	17	0/0	244	0.3/1
Sour cream	64	6/84	291	6.3/20
Sour cream, low-fat	50	0.4/72	277	4.3/14
Sour cream, nonfat	35	0/0	262	0.3/1
Yogurt, low-fat	16	0.4/23	234	0.7/3
Yogurt, nonfat	15	0/0	242	0.3/1

> *"My idea of Heaven is a great big baked potato and someone to share it with."*
>
> —OPRAH WINFREY

✳ Beacon Club Broccoli Salad ✳

This is a favorite salad in Kalamazoo and has become the best way I know of to eat loads of broccoli.

SERVES 4

6 cups broccoli florets (1 to 1 1/2 pounds)
1/2 cup coarsely chopped red onion
8 cherry tomatoes, halved
1/2 cup orange juice
3 tablespoons red wine vinegar
2 tablespoons light brown sugar
1 tablespoon finely minced orange zest
2 tablespoons olive oil

1. Put the broccoli in a large steaming basket and steam over 1 inch of boiling water for 3 to 5 minutes, until tender but still crunchy. Drain and rinse immediately with cold water to stop the cooking. Transfer to a bowl and toss with the onion and tomatoes.
2. In a small bowl, combine the orange juice, vinegar, sugar, and orange zest. Slowly whisk in the oil until well blended. Dress the broccoli with 1/3 cup of dressing and toss well. (Reserve the remaining dressing for future use.) Chill the salad for 1 hour before serving.

Cal. 147   Carb. 20g   Prot. 4g   Chol. 0mg   Fat 7g/41%   Sod. 42mg

VEGETABLES AU NATUREL

One of the smartest ways to cut fat is to stop putting it on vegetables. It's amazing how fresh steamed asparagus, broccoli, green beans, and zucchini taste unadorned. They're really quite addictive, but if you want to add flavor, consider the following options:

SEASONING (1 TABLESPOON)	CAL.	FAT (G)/%
Brown sugar	34	0/0
Butter	102	12/100
Fresh herbs	1	0/0
Hollandaise	44	4/88
Olive oil	119	14/100
Parmesan cheese	29	2/62
Rice wine vinegar	15	0/0
Sliced almonds	35	3/77

* Black Bean Quesadillas *

Layers of powerful flavors ooze together to make each bite delicious.

SERVES 2

1/2 cup cooked or canned black beans, drained
1 tablespoon finely minced garlic
1 teaspoon low-fat, low-sodium chicken broth
2 tablespoons finely minced fresh cilantro
1/4 cup low-fat goat cheese
1/3 cup nonfat cottage cheese
Salt and freshly ground black pepper to taste
2 large flour tortillas (about 10 inches)
1 cup washed, stemmed, coarsely chopped fresh spinach
1/4 cup finely minced red onion
1/2 cup salsa (mild, medium, or hot) or 1/2 cup Pico de Gallo (recipe follows)
1/4 cup grated part-skim mozzarella

1. Preheat the oven to 425°F. In a small bowl, combine the beans, garlic, broth, and cilantro. Using a fork, crush the beans slightly and set aside.
2. In a blender or using an immersion blender, blend the goat cheese and cottage cheese until smooth. Season with salt and pepper and set aside.
3. Spread half of the bean mixture over each tortilla and top with half of the cheese mixture.
4. Sprinkle each tortilla with spinach, onion, and salsa. Place one tortilla on a baking sheet and position the other on top of it. Sprinkle with mozzarella and bake for about 12 minutes, or until bubbling and heated through. Serve immediately.

Cal. 342   Carb. 50g   Prot. 20g   Chol. 18mg   Fat 7.8g/20%   Sod. 620mg

PICO DE GALLO

Here's a salsa that disappears quickly.

MAKES 2 CUPS

1¹/₂ cups coarsely chopped tomatoes
¹/₄ cup coarsely chopped onion
¹/₄ teaspoon sugar
1 seeded and finely minced jalapeño
1 tablespoon plus 2 teaspoons fresh lime juice
¹/₂ cup finely minced fresh cilantro

In a large mixing bowl, combine all of the ingredients. Cover and chill for at least 1 hour before serving.

Cal. 1.5   Carb. 0.4g   Prot. 0.05g   Chol. 0mg   Fat 0g/0%   Sod. 10mg
(analyzed per tablespoon)

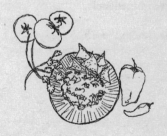

* Blue Cheese–Stuffed Potatoes *

If you love blue-veined cheeses, as I do, it's amazing how far just a little bit of Roquefort goes.

SERVES 2

Two 10-ounce baking potatoes, washed, dried, and pierced
   several times with a fork
1 tablespoon Roquefort cheese
$1/3$ cup plus 2 tablespoons Nonfat Blend (recipe follows)
4 tablespoons finely minced fresh chives
$1/2$ cup coarsely chopped arugula
Freshly ground black pepper to taste

1. Preheat the oven to 500°F.
2. Lay the potatoes on the oven rack and bake for 1 hour, until tender. Cool.
3. Halve the potatoes lengthwise. Carefully scoop out the insides and transfer to a bowl. Add the cheese, Nonfat Blend, chives, and arugula and mash with a fork. Season with pepper.
4. Carefully stuff the potato mixture back into the skins. Set on a baking sheet lined with aluminum foil and bake for an additional 30 minutes, until heated through and lightly browned. Serve immediately.

Cal. 344   Carb. 74g   Prot. 10g   Chol. 3mg   Fat 2g/4%   Sod. 93mg

NONFAT BLEND

At the beginning of every week, I whip up a batch of this in the blender. (I never use the food processor; its power breaks down the mixture and makes it watery.) I stash it in a plastic container in the fridge to use by the cup or spoonful in myriad ways as the week progresses. You'll find it used throughout as a replacement for sour cream, mayonnaise, or heavy cream.

MAKES ABOUT 2 CUPS

1 cup nonfat plain yogurt
1 cup nonfat cottage cheese

In a blender, combine the yogurt and cottage cheese and blend until smooth. Transfer to a container, cover, and refrigerate for up to 1 week.

Cal. 9.3   Carb. 0.9g   Prot. 1.3g   Chol. 0.14mg   Fat 0g/0%   Sod. 33.3mg
(analyzed per tablespoon)

* Braised Leeks *

I make these leeks in the microwave rather than braising them on top of the stove.

SERVES 4

1 pound leeks, cut in half lengthwise
2 teaspoons low-fat, low-sodium chicken broth
2 tablespoons brown sugar

1. Put the leeks in a glass dish and add the chicken broth. Cover tightly and microwave on high for 6 to 8 minutes.
2. Uncover, sprinkle with the brown sugar, cover, turning back at corner to vent, and then microwave for 2 minutes on high. Toss to coat and serve immediately.

Cal. 53   Carb. 13.1g   Prot. 1.01g   Chol. 0mg   Fat 0.23g/3%   Sod. 31mg

❋ Caesar Salad with Pepper Croutons ❋

Over the years, I've lightened this classic many times. I like it to have a creamy, lemon-cheese flavor, and I never even *miss* the anchovies, egg, or oil!

SERVES 4

8 firmly packed cups romaine lettuce, torn into bite-size pieces
1 cup Pepper Croutons (recipe follows)
1/4 cup nonfat cottage cheese
1/2 cup nonfat plain yogurt
2 tablespoons lemon juice, or to taste
4 teaspoons finely minced garlic
1/4 cup grated Parmesan cheese
Salt and freshly ground black pepper to taste
Twelve 3-inch Parmesan shards (see page 24)

1. Place the lettuce and Pepper Croutons in a salad bowl.
2. In a blender, process the cottage cheese until smooth.
3. In a small mixing bowl, combine the cottage cheese, yogurt, lemon juice, garlic, and grated Parmesan cheese. Mix until blended, taste, and adjust seasonings.
4. Toss the lettuce and croutons with 1/4 cup of the dressing until well coated. (Refrigerate the remaining dressing in a tightly lidded jar.) Season with salt and pepper. Divide the salad onto 4 large plates, top each with 3 Parmesan shards and serve immediately.

NOTE: Use the leftover dressing within the next week.

Cal. 218   Carb. 29g   Prot. 16g   Chol. 14mg   Fat 6.5g/25%   Sod. 546mg

PARMESAN SHARDS

To get long, broad curls or shards of Parmesan, peel with a vegetable peeler as you would a potato. Always invest in the *real* aged Parmigiano-Reggiano. Its sweet nutty flavor is well worth it. Sixteen 3-inch Parmesan shards equal about $1/4$ cup.

PEPPER CROUTONS

Use the best quality multigrain bread you can buy. I suggest buying it at a good local bakery—or bake it yourself!

MAKES ABOUT 4 CUPS

1 teaspoon freshly ground black pepper
$1/2$ teaspoon crushed red pepper flakes
4 cups cubed multigrain bread (5 to 6 slices)

1. Preheat the oven to 425°F.
2. In a small bowl, mix the black pepper and red pepper flakes. Spread the bread on a baking sheet and spray lightly with olive oil spray. Sprinkle with the pepper mixture and toss to coat evenly. Bake for 10 to 15 minutes, tossing every 2 to 3 minutes, until browned, crisp, and dry. Allow to cool completely before using. Store in an airtight container.

Cal. 231˝ Carb. 58g   Prot. 11.5g.   Chol. 0mg   Fat 0.009g/1%   Sod. 777mg
(analyzed per $1/2$ cup)

✳ Carrots Rapée ✳

This French bistro classic is usually dressed with a vinai-
grette with quite a bit of oil. I think it's improved when
sparked with citrus juices and mint.

SERVES 2

1 cup grated carrots
3 tablespoons dried currants
1 tablespoon orange juice
¹/₂ teaspoon finely minced orange zest
2 teaspoons lemon juice
2 teaspoons finely minced fresh mint

1. In a mixing bowl, combine the carrots and currants. Set
aside.
2. In another bowl, combine the orange juice, orange zest,
and lemon juice. Toss with the carrot mixture. Add the
mint, toss, and refrigerate for at least 1 hour, or until ready
to serve.

Cal. 35   Carb. 8.8g   Prot. 1g   Chol. 0mg   Fat 0.1g/3%   Sod. 20mg

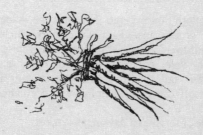

CARROT POWER

Carotene gives carrots and pumpkins their cheerful orange-yellow hue. Just one carrot provides twice the RDA of anti-oxidant beta-carotene, thought to help delay cataracts and reduce the risk of heart disease. Available preshredded at the supermarket, carrots are easy to add to soups, tomato sauces, rice dishes, salads, and stuffing.

Other deep orange vegetables and fruits and dark green leafy vegetables are rich sources of beta-carotene, too:

* Apricots
* Sweet red peppers
* Broccoli
* Brussels sprouts
* Cabbage
* Beet greens
* Mustard greens
* Kale
* Spinach
* Sweet potatoes
* Tomatoes
* Winter squash

CABBAGE AND CANCER

Vegetables with flower petals that form the shape of a cross are called "cruciferous." Family members—including cabbage, cauliflower, Brussels sprouts, watercress, broccoli, horseradish, kale, kohlrabi, mustard, radishes, rutabaga, turnip, Asian and collard greens—all contain a chemical that wards off cancer by helping detoxify cancer-causing agents.

A couple of servings a day are all it takes.

* Creamy Cucumber Salad *

SERVES 8

¹/₄ cup nonfat plain yogurt
2 tablespoons nonfat sour cream
2 teaspoons lemon juice
4 teaspoons finely minced fresh mint
4 cups very thinly sliced cucumber

In a small mixing bowl, combine the yogurt, sour cream, lemon juice, and mint and mix well. Add the cucumber and toss. Cover and refrigerate for at least 1 hour before serving to allow flavors to blend.

Cal. 14   Carb. 3g   Prot. 1.1g   Chol. 0.1mg   Fat 0.1g/5%   Sod. 9mg

DRESSING BASES FOR CREAMY SALADS

Once you try to reduce or eliminate mayonnaise, only your own taste buds can decide which of the following you would choose to spend your fat allowance on.

1 TABLESPOON	CAL.	FAT (G)/%
Mayonnaise	99	11/100
Low-calorie mayonnaise	36	3/75
Fat-free mayonnaise	11	0/0
Nonfat Blend (see page 21)	9	0/0
Nonfat cottage cheese	9	0/0
Nonfat yogurt	8	0/0

✻ Creamy Guacamole ✻

Finally, there's a guacamole that lets us dip into it with some abandon. Others can be 97 percent fat!

MAKES ABOUT 2 CUPS

$^1/_4$ *cup Nonfat Blend (see page 21)*
$^1/_2$ *avocado, peeled*
$^1/_2$ *cup finely chopped red onion*
2 cups finely chopped tomatoes
1 tablespoon seeded and finely minced jalapeño
1 tablespoon finely minced garlic
2 tablespoons lime juice
$^1/_4$ *cup finely minced cilantro*
1 tablespoon finely minced lime zest
Dash of Tabasco

In a blender or using an immersion blender, combine the Nonfat Blend and avocado until smooth. Transfer to a bowl, add the remaining ingredients, and mix well. Cover with plastic wrap and refrigerate for at least 1 hour before serving.

Cal. 3 Carb. 0.4g Prot. 0.1g Chol. 0mg Fat 0.1g/30% Sod. 0.06mg
(analyzed per teaspoon)

* Delightful Dips *

LEMON-PEPPER DIP

MAKES ABOUT 1 CUP

1 cup nonfat cottage cheese
3 tablespoons finely minced fresh dill
1 teaspoon finely minced lemon zest
$1/2$ teaspoon lemon juice
$1/2$ teaspoon freshly ground black pepper

In a blender, process the cottage cheese until smooth. Transfer to a bowl; add the dill, lemon zest, lemon juice, and pepper and mix well. Cover and refrigerate for 1 to 2 hours before serving to allow the flavors to blend.

Cal. 3   Carb. 0.2g   Prot. 0.6g   Chol. 0mg   Fat 0g/0%   Sod. 18mg

(analyzed per teaspoon)

SPINACH DIP

MAKES ABOUT 1 1/2 CUPS

1 cup nonfat cottage cheese
3 tablespoons nonfat plain yogurt
1 cup frozen spinach, thawed and squeezed of excess water
1 teaspoon finely minced garlic
1 tablespoon grated Parmesan cheese
Freshly ground nutmeg to taste
Freshly ground black pepper to taste

In a blender, process the cottage cheese until smooth. Transfer to a bowl; add the yogurt, spinach, garlic, Parmesan cheese, nutmeg, and pepper and mix well. Cover and refrigerate for 1 to 2 hours before serving to allow the flavors to blend.

Cal. 4   Carb. 0.3g   Prot. 0.5g   Chol. 0.1mg   Fat 0.03g/6%   Sod. 16mg
(analyzed per teaspoon)

ROASTED PEPPER DIP

MAKES ABOUT 1 1/4 CUPS

1 cup nonfat cottage cheese
1 red or orange bell pepper, roasted, seeded, and peeled
  (instructions follow)
1 teaspoon finely minced garlic
Dash of cayenne or Tabasco sauce to taste

In a blender, process the ingredients until smooth. Cover and refrigerate for 1 to 2 hours to allow the flavors to blend.

Cal. 3   Carb. 3g   Prot. 0.5g   Chol. 0mg   Fat 0g/1%   Sod. 15mg
(analyzed per teaspoon)

ROASTING PEPPERS

Roasting red, yellow, orange, and purple bell peppers imbues them with a flavor that is smoky and intense—and a soft, rich, velvety texture.

To roast: Preheat the broiler. Cut the peppers in half, removing the seeds and membranes. For a more evenly charred skin, cut slits every 1 to 2 inches around the circumference of the peppers to allow them to lie flat. Place under the broiler, skin side up, 2 to 3 inches from the heat. Rotate until blackened all over, 8 to 12 minutes. Transfer the peppers to a paper or plastic bag, close, and allow to sweat for 15 to 20 minutes. Remove from bag and gently peel away the charred skin. Store covered and refrigerated for up to a week. Be sure to make use of the lovely natural juices that collect.

ROQUEFORT DIP

MAKES ABOUT 1 1/4 CUPS

1 cup nonfat cottage cheese
3 tablespoons crumbled Roquefort cheese

In a blender, process the cottage cheese until smooth.
Transfer to a bowl, add the Roquefort, and stir well until
tinged lightly with pale green from the cheese. Cover and
refrigerate for 1 to 2 hours before serving to allow the flavors
to blend.

Cal. 4   Carb. 0.2g   Prot. 0.6g   Chol. 0.3mg   Fat 0.1g/27%   Sod. 20mg

(analyzed per teaspoon)

PESTO DIP

MAKES ABOUT 1 CUP

1 cup nonfat cottage cheese
2 tablespoons Spinach Pesto (see page 79)

In a blender, process the cottage cheese until smooth.
Transfer to a bowl, add the Spinach Pesto, and mix well.
Cover and refrigerate for 1 to 2 hours before serving to allow
the flavors to blend.

Cal. 4   Carb. 0.2g   Prot. 0.7g   Chol. 0 mg   Fat 0.045g/10%   Sod. 18mg

(analyzed per teaspoon)

SHRIMP DIP

MAKES ABOUT 1 1/2 CUPS

1 cup nonfat cottage cheese
1 cup cooked large shrimp, cut into chunks (about 14 shrimp)
1 tablespoon lemon juice
2 tablespoons finely minced fresh dill
1 to 2 dashes of Tabasco sauce

In a blender, process all the ingredients until almost smooth. Cover and refrigerate for 1 to 2 hours before serving to allow the flavors to blend.

Cal. 3.4   Carb. 0.2g   Prot. 0.6g   Chol. 2mg   Fat 0.01g/4%   Sod. 15mg
(analyzed per teaspoon)

SUN-DRIED TOMATO DIP

MAKES ABOUT 1 1/2 CUPS

1 cup nonfat cottage cheese
1/4 cup oil-packed sun-dried tomatoes, drained
1 tablespoon finely minced scallions, green part only
1 teaspoon finely minced garlic
1 teaspoon tomato paste
2 tablespoons crumbled feta cheese

In a blender, process the cottage cheese, tomatoes, scallions, garlic, and tomato paste until smooth. Transfer to a bowl, add the feta, and mix well. Cover and refrigerate for 2 hours before serving to give the flavors time to blend.

Cal. 4   Carb. 0.3g   Prot. 0.5g   Chol. 0.4mg   Fat 0.14g/30%   Sod. 18mg

(analyzed per teaspoon)

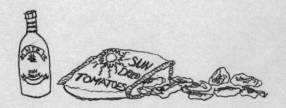

CRAB DIP

MAKES ABOUT 1 1/2 CUPS

1 cup nonfat cottage cheese
1 cup cooked crabmeat
1/2 cup finely chopped scallions, green part only
1/4 teaspoon Worcestershire sauce
1/2 teaspoon bottled cocktail sauce

In a blender, process the cottage cheese until smooth. Transfer to a bowl; add the crabmeat, scallions, Worcestershire sauce, and cocktail sauce and mix. Cover and refrigerate for 1 to 2 hours before serving to allow the flavors to blend.

Cal. 4   Carb. 0.2g   Prot. 0.7g   Chol. 1.6mg   Fat 0.03g/7%   Sod. 17mg
(analyzed per teaspoon)

* Flavored Liquids for Steaming Vegetables *

In this section I have assembled eight lightly flavored liquids that will make steamed vegetables really come alive—without adding a single calorie or gram of fat. Combine the ingredients for the liquids in the bottom part of a vegetable steamer and use them to steam fresh vegetables. Not only will they fill the kitchen with a tantalizing aroma, they will gently infuse the vegetables with flavor you never thought possible. Then just savor them.

CITRUS

MAKES 2 CUPS

Juice of 1 lemon
Juice of 1 lime
Juice of 1 orange
$^1/_2$ cup minced fresh mint
$1^1/_2$ cups water

MEXICAN

MAKES $2^1/_4$ CUPS

1 whole jalapeño, sliced
Juice and zest of 1 lemon
2 cups water

LIME-GARLIC

MAKES 3 CUPS

10 cloves garlic, halved
2 limes, in $^1/_8$-inch slices
2 bay leaves
2 teaspoons peppercorns
3 cups water

ASIAN

MAKES $2^1/_2$ CUPS

$^1/_4$ cup soy sauce
3 tablespoons chopped fresh ginger
$^1/_4$ cup coarsely chopped garlic
2 cups water

ITALIAN

MAKES 2 CUPS

2 tablespoons coarsely
    chopped garlic
1 cup basil
2 cups water

INDIAN

MAKES 3 CUPS

3 tablespoons Dijon mustard
2 tablespoons curry powder
3 cups water

GINGER

MAKES 3 CUPS

One 3-inch piece fresh ginger,
    peeled and cut into chunks
2 tablespoons dry mustard
3 cups water

AUTUMN

MAKES 1$\frac{1}{2}$ CUPS

1 teaspoon cinnamon
2 teaspoons whole cloves
1$\frac{1}{2}$ cups water

"Tomatoes and oregano make it Italian; wine and tarragon make it French. Sour cream makes it Russian; lemon and cinnamon make it Greek. Soy sauce makes it Chinese; garlic makes it good."

—ALICE MAY BROCK

✷ Fluffy Mashed Potatoes ✷

To this basic recipe you could add several minced garlic cloves, basil, low-fat pesto, nonfat sour cream, nonfat cream cheese, fresh dill, Italian parsley, or chives—just about anything to suit your own taste!

SERVES 4 GENEROUSLY

4 medium russet (baking) potatoes, peeled and quartered
²/₃ cup skim milk (or more, depending on the stiffness you prefer), warmed
Salt and freshly ground black pepper to taste

1. Place the potatoes in a saucepan and cover with water. Boil over medium-high heat for 25 to 30 minutes, until the potatoes begin to fall apart. Drain.
2. Mash the potatoes with a hand mixer until smooth. Add the milk, ¹/₃ cup at a time, beating well after each addition, until the potatoes are fluffy. Season with salt and pepper, mix, taste, and adjust the seasonings. Serve immediately.

Cal. 102   Carb. 22g   Prot. 4g   Chol. 0.7mg   Fat 0.2g/2%   Sod. 26mg

* Gazpacho Salad *

By leaving the Spanish soup chunky, I have created a salad
filled with zippy flavor—an idea borrowed from the original
Settlement Cookbook.

SERVES 4

2 small cucumbers, sliced very thin
4 scallions, white bulb and 3 inches of green, coarsely chopped
4 plum tomatoes, cut into bite-size pieces
1 orange or yellow bell pepper, seeds and membrane removed,
    diced (about $1/2$ cup)
$1/4$ cup finely minced Italian parsley
2 tablespoons finely minced garlic
1 cup low-sodium tomato juice
2 teaspoons red wine vinegar
Dash of Tabasco sauce
Salt and freshly ground black pepper to taste
4 cups dark green leaves (such as spinach, watercress, or
    arugula), washed, stemmed, and dried

1. In a medium bowl, combine the cucumbers, scallions,
tomatoes, pepper, and parsley and toss lightly.
2. In a small bowl, combine the garlic, tomato juice, vinegar,
and Tabasco and mix with a fork. Season with salt and
pepper.
3. Drizzle the dressing over the salad and toss well. Divide
the greens among 4 salad plates, top with the dressed vegetables, and serve immediately.

Cal. 70   Carb. 15g   Prot. 4g   Chol. 0mg   Fat 0.6g/7.7%   Sod. 194mg

✳ Ginger Carrots ✳

Although similar recipes rely on butter, I've substituted water to melt the brown sugar and coat the carrots.

SERVES 2

1/2 pound baby carrots, peeled and cleaned
1/2 teaspoon ground ginger
2 tablespoons light brown sugar
1 tablespoon water
1/2 teaspoon caraway seeds

1. In a medium saucepan, cover the carrots with water. Cook, covered, over medium-high heat for 10 to 12 minutes, or until tender.
2. Meanwhile, in a small bowl, combine the ginger, sugar, and water.
3. Drain the carrots and return to the pan. Add the sugar water and toss well. Cook over medium heat for 2 to 3 minutes, until the carrots are well coated. Add the caraway seeds, toss, and serve immediately.

Cal. 88   Carb. 21g   Prot. 1g   Chol. 0mg   Fat 0.3g/3%   Sod. 78mg

* Ginger Green Beans *

This is a favorite Chinese-style vegetable of mine, pared down to have a minimum of fat.

SERVES 6

1 tablespoon olive oil
1 tablespoon plus 1 1/2 teaspoons finely minced fresh ginger
1 tablespoon finely minced garlic
1 1/2 pounds green beans, trimmed
1 1/2 cups low-fat, low-sodium chicken broth
Freshly ground black pepper to taste

1. In a large skillet, heat the olive oil over medium heat. Add the ginger and garlic and cook for about 1 minute, until lightly browned.
2. Add the beans and cook for 2 to 3 minutes, stirring constantly. Add the chicken broth and continue cooking, tossing, for about 5 minutes, until the liquid evaporates and the beans are tender. Season with pepper and serve immediately.

Cal. 62 Carb. 9g Prot. 3g Chol. 0mg Fat 2.4g/31% Sod. 147mg

✱ Green Beans with Roasted Red Peppers ✱

Smoky red peppers add immense sparkle atop dark green beans!

SERVES 4

1 pound green beans
2 tablespoons finely minced fresh basil
¼ cup finely chopped roasted red pepper (see page 31)
Salt and freshly ground black pepper to taste

1. Put the green beans in a steaming basket set over 2 inches of boiling water and steam for 5 to 7 minutes, until tender.
2. Transfer the beans to a bowl and toss with the basil and peppers. Lightly spray with olive oil spray and toss to coat evenly. Season with salt and pepper and serve immediately.

Cal. 38   Carb. 8.6g   Prot. 2g   Chol. 0mg   Fat 0.2g/3%   Sod. 104mg

> "Have you seen a red sunset drip over one of my cornfields?"
>
> —CARL SANDBURG

* Green Green Beans *

Parsley really does make green beans taste greener.

SERVES 4

2 pounds green beans, ends snapped
1 teaspoon finely minced garlic
3 tablespoons finely minced Italian parsley
Freshly ground black pepper to taste

1. Put the beans in a large skillet and cover with ¹/₂ inch of water. Cover and cook over medium-high heat for 4 to 6 minutes, until crisp-tender. Drain. You may have to do this in batches.
2. In a large bowl, toss the beans with the garlic, parsley, and pepper. Serve immediately.

Cal. 96   Carb. 13g   Prot. 3g   Chol. 0mg   Fat 0.4g/3%   Sod. 11mg

JAZZ UP SALADS

Add to simple greens:

- Kohlrabi
- Fennel
- Roasted peppers
- Pineapple chunks
- Sprouts
- Mushrooms
- Sweet onions
- Capers
- Green peppercorns
- Ginger (candied or fresh)
- Raisins
- Apples
- Green beans
- Radishes
- Water chestnuts
- Broccoli
- Pea pods
- Berries
- Pears
- Daikon radish
- Sugar snap peas
- Shredded carrots
- Grated red cabbage

* Herbed Bruschetta *

An Italian favorite you can create at home. This is a lovely tasting version of the Tuscan classic. In summer, this dish praises the glories of the tomato harvest. And if you use very ripe plum tomatoes, you can enjoy it during the remainder of the year, too.

MAKES 12 SLICES

1/4 cup finely chopped fresh Italian parsley
1/4 cup drained capers, chopped
2 teaspoons finely minced fresh tarragon
Salt and freshly ground black pepper to taste
1 tablespoon extra-virgin olive oil
1 large ripe tomato, finely diced
2 tablespoons finely minced fresh mint
Twelve 1/4-inch-thick slices peasant bread or French bread.

1. In a bowl, combine the parsley, capers, tarragon, and salt and pepper. Add the oil and toss well. Set aside.
2. Put the tomato in another bowl and season with salt and pepper. Add the mint. Let stand at room temperature for at least 1 hour.
3. Toast or grill the bread slices.
4. Spread the oil mixture on the warm toast and top each with the tomato mixture. Serve immediately.

Cal. 91   Carb. 16g   Prot. 3g   Chol. 0mg   Fat 1.8g/18%   Sod. 252mg

(analyzed per slice)

FIELD OF GREENS

Forget ho-hum salads! There's a wealth of salad greens available.

- Belgian endive
- Boston lettuce
- Chinese cabbage
- Chicory
- Bibb lettuce
- Escarole
- Green cabbage
- Frisée
- Iceberg lettuce
- Arugula
- Beet greens
- Mâche
- Mesclun
- Mustard greens
- Romaine lettuce
- Chard
- Cress
- Kale
- Radicchio
- Spinach
- Pea shoots

* Herbed Scalloped Potatoes *

These are pleasingly moist and loaded with flavor.

SERVES 4

1 pound Yukon Gold or russet potatoes, peeled and thinly sliced
1 tablespoon finely minced fresh thyme
4 fresh or dried bay leaves
2 tablespoons crumbled goat cheese
1 cup skim milk
2 tablespoons instant potato flakes
Freshly ground black pepper

1. Preheat the oven to 350°F.
2. Lay half the potatoes in an 8 × 8 × 2-inch casserole. Sprinkle 1¹/₂ teaspoons thyme over the potatoes and then layer with the remaining potatoes. Nestle the bay leaves into the potatoes.
3. In a blender, combine the cheese, ¹/₄ cup milk, and the potato flakes and blend until smooth. Add the remaining ³/₄ cup milk and blend to combine. Pour over the potatoes, sprinkle with the remaining 1¹/₂ teaspoons thyme, and season to taste with the pepper. Cover tightly with foil and bake for 45 minutes. Uncover and bake for about 20 minutes longer, until the potatoes are fork-tender and lightly browned. Remove and discard the bay leaves.

Cal. 139   Carb. 25g   Prot. 6g   Chol. 5mg   Fat 2g/13%   Sod. 67mg

FRESH BAY LEAVES

Since I moved to Michigan, I've nurtured six 8-foot topiary bay trees planted in big terra-cotta pots. In winter, they line a bright wall in my cottage office. But come spring, we set them out in the garden, where they stand in a row like Roman sentinels.

I can't tell you how much their fresh, fragrant, almost citruslike presence has added to my cooking, enhancing sauces, stews, and soups as you might expect, but also rice dishes, poached fish, vegetable dishes, even savory custards.

They require a minimum of care—water and moderate sunlight. Clipping leaves for cooking takes care of the pruning. They can grow to be forty feet tall.

It's lovely how they contribute as much to cooking as they do to fragrant summer walks in the garden.

> *"Years may wrinkle the skin, but to give up enthusiasm wrinkles the soul."*
>
> —SAMUEL ULLMAN

* Hobo Potatoes *

This campfire specialty is brought indoors without any butter!

SERVES 6

12 medium russet potatoes, washed and thinly sliced
3 medium red onions, thinly sliced, rings separated
2 tablespoons finely minced garlic
1¹/₂ teaspoons finely minced fresh tarragon or sage
Salt and freshly ground black pepper to taste

1. Preheat the oven to 350°F.
2. Lay six 12 × 18-inch sheets of aluminum foil on the countertop and divide the potatoes, onion, garlic, and herbs among the sheets. Season with salt and pepper.
3. Cover each with another sheet of foil and fold into 6 tight packages. Transfer to two baking sheets and bake for about 45 minutes, until the potatoes are fork-tender. Take care when opening the foil packages; the escaping steam is hot. Remove the potatoes to a serving plate and serve immediately.

Cal. 202   Carb. 46g   Prot. 5.5g   Chol. 0mg   Fat 0.3g/1%   Sod. 16mg

* Honey Mustard Beets *

I love oven-roasted fresh beets, but to beat the clock I will use canned in a pinch.

SERVES 8

8 cups thinly sliced cooked or canned beets, drained
³/₄ cup finely minced fresh chives
¹/₂ cup finely minced fresh Italian parsley
2 tablespoons plus 2 teaspoons Dijon mustard
¹/₂ cup honey
4 teaspoons balsamic vinegar
Freshly ground black pepper to taste
¹/₂ cup walnut pieces, toasted

1. In a large bowl, combine the beets, chives, and parsley.
2. In another bowl, combine the mustard, honey, and vinegar and stir until smooth. Toss with the beet mixture to coat and then season with pepper. Sprinkle with walnuts. Set aside for 1 to 2 hours at room temperature before serving to give the flavors time to blend.

NOTE: To toast walnut pieces and other nuts, spread them on a baking sheet and bake in a preheated 350°F oven for 5 to 8 minutes, until lightly browned and fragrant. Stir 2 to 3 times during toasting. Transfer to a plate to cool.

Cal. 156   Carb. 27g   Prot. 3g   Chol. 0mg   Fat 5.5g/29%   Sod. 579mg

GREAT GREENS

The variety of greens available in the United States seems to multiply from day to day. Don't let them intimidate you. Pass them up and you'll miss all the fun!

When in doubt, take a leafy stranger home for dinner. Toss some into a simple salad. To taste it warm, sauté in a bit of olive oil and chicken broth. Stir-fry. Wilt it as a bed for fish or simmer it in soup.

Bok choy: This has white stems and green leaves—both are delicate and edible. Look for baby bok choy.

Chinese cabbage: Barrel-shaped napa and more elongated michihili are mild and crunchy.

Choy sum: Slightly bitter, the stems are more tender than the leaves. The tiny yellow flowers are edible, too.

Green mustard: There are many varieties, with leaves of different shapes. The flavor is always pungent.

Mizuna: It's called "water vegetable" because the stalks are very juicy. Use baby leaves in salads; mature ones are better cooked.

Pea shoots: These are the tendrils and top few leaves of the snow pea plant. The delicate pea flavor comes through raw, steamed, or stir-fried.

Red mustard: The flavor is similar to hot wasabi.

Tatsoi: This is a ground-hugging member of the bok choy family, with thick dark green leaves that grow like rose petals. Slightly bitter, it's great raw. It adds sparkle to soups when tossed in at the last minute.

* Individual Eggplant Towers *

Here's a lighter version of the Italian classic Eggplant Parmigiana.

SERVES 4

2 small eggplants, cut horizontally into six 1/2-inch slices
3/4 cup Quick Tomato Sauce (see page 58)
3/4 cup grated part-skim mozzarella
2 tablespoons finely minced garlic
4 tablespoons finely minced fresh Italian parsley
4 tablespoons grated Parmesan cheese
4 tablespoons finely minced fresh basil

1. Preheat the oven to 400°F. Spray 2 baking sheets with olive oil spray. Lay the eggplant slices on the sheets in a single layer and bake until fork-tender (about 10 minutes on each side), spraying the eggplant when you flip it. Cool for about 10 minutes.
2. Spray a baking sheet with olive oil spray and place 4 slices of eggplant on it. Begin layering—each individual tower has 3 identical layers: 1 tablespoon sauce, 1 tablespoon mozzarella, 1/2 teaspoon garlic, 1 teaspoon parsley, 1 teaspoon Parmesan, 1 teaspoon basil. Repeat twice. Bake, uncovered, for 25 to 30 minutes, until the cheese is golden brown.

Cal. 144   Carb. 11g   Prot. 10g   Chol. 16.4mg   Fat 5.7g/36%   Sod. 395mg

* One-Two-Three-Potatoes *

These crispy potatoes are loaded with golden garlic and require no effort at all! I love them!

SERVES 4

1 pound small russet potatoes, quartered
1 tablespoon plus 1 teaspoon olive oil
¹/₄ cup finely minced garlic
2 tablespoons chopped fresh parsley
Salt and freshly ground black pepper to taste

1. Preheat the oven to 375°F.
2. Place the potatoes in a 9 × 12-inch baking dish and toss with the oil. Roast for 25 minutes, stirring several times. Add the garlic, toss, and cook for 5 to 10 minutes, until the garlic is tender and beginning to brown.
3. Toss with the parsley, season with salt and pepper, and serve immediately.

Cal. 153   Carb. 26g   Prot. 3g   Chol. 0mg   Fat 4.6g/27%   Sod. 10mg

* Our House Dressing *

I've always preferred a dressing that is more acidic than oily. I keep this on hand to toss with greens and pasta, sprinkle on sandwiches, or glaze vegetables, meats, or poultry as they grill. Be sure to use balsamic vinegar from Modena, which is sharper when young and becomes sweeter, more caramelized, and viscous as it ages. Don't worry about the hot water—it works.

MAKES ³/₄ CUP

2 teaspoons finely minced garlic
1 tablespoon Dijon mustard
¹/₂ cup balsamic vinegar
¹/₄ cup hot water
1 tablespoon sugar
1 tablespoon olive oil
Salt and freshly ground black pepper to taste

1. In a small bowl, combine the garlic and mustard and mix well. Whisk in the balsamic vinegar, hot water, and sugar. Taste the dressing; the sugar should take the edge off the vinegar.
2. Slowly add the olive oil, whisking continuously, until emulsified. Season with salt and pepper. Use immediately or cover and refrigerate.

Cal. 18   Carb. 2g   Prot. 0.1g   Chol. 0mg   Fat 1.2g/58%   Sod. 31mg
(analyzed per tablespoon)

* Oven-Fried Cottage Potatoes *

These are easy, easy, easy—and so satisfying!

SERVES 2

2 Yukon Gold or russet potatoes, peeled and sliced thin

1. Soak the potato slices in ice water for 1 hour.
2. Preheat the oven to 450°F about 15 minutes before draining the potatoes.
3. Drain and pat the potatoes dry with paper towels. Spread on a baking sheet and lightly spray with olive oil spray. Bake for 30 minutes, tossing every 5 minutes, until crispy and golden. Serve immediately.

Cal. 111   Carb. 25.3g   Prot. 2.9g   Chol. 0mg   Fat 1.4g/1%   Sod. 8.4mg

* Oven-Fried Vegetables *

These are fantastic with Lemon-Pepper Dip (see page 29) or just a squeeze or two of lemon.

SERVES 4

1 cup plain bread crumbs or Panko (see page 12)
1 teaspoon garlic powder
$1/2$ teaspoon paprika
4 large egg whites
16 to 20 large button mushrooms, stemmed
20 broccoli florets
12 to 16 cauliflower florets

1. Preheat the oven to 450°F.
2. In a plastic bag, combine the bread crumbs, garlic powder, and paprika. In a shallow bowl, lightly beat the egg whites with a fork.
3. Coat the vegetables, a few at a time, in the egg whites and then drop into the bag of crumbs and shake to coat. Shake off any excess crumbs and lay the vegetables on a baking sheet. Repeat until all the vegetables are coated. Spray lightly with olive oil spray and bake for 30 minutes, tossing every 10 minutes, until vegetables are crispy and lightly browned. Serve immediately.

Cal. 167   Carb. 29g   Prot. 11g   Chol. 2mg   Fat 2g/10%   Sod. 310mg

* Quick Tomato Sauce *

This is a fresh-tasting, chunky tomato sauce that can be made any time of year. It freezes very well, which is lucky because it's great to have on hand.

MAKES 5¹/₂ CUPS

1 tablespoon low-fat, low-sodium chicken broth
¹/₄ cup finely minced garlic
1 cup coarsely chopped onion
Two 28-ounce cans plum tomatoes plus the juice from 1 can
1 teaspoon dried oregano
3 tablespoons tomato paste
Salt and freshly ground black pepper to taste
3 tablespoons finely minced fresh Italian parsley

1. In a large saucepan, heat the chicken broth over low flame. Add the garlic and onion and cook, stirring, for 4 to 5 minutes, until translucent. Stir in a little more broth if necessary to prevent sticking. Add the tomatoes, tomato juice, oregano, and tomato paste.
2. Simmer gently over medium heat, uncovered, for about 30 minutes, stirring occasionally and using the spoon to break the tomatoes into smaller pieces. Season with salt and pepper and add the parsley. Use immediately or cover and refrigerate until needed.

Cal. 19   Carb. 4.5g   Prot. 1.2g   Chol. 0mg   Fat 0.05g/2%   Sod. 215mg
(analyzed per ¹/₄ cup)

✳ Ratatouille Sandwich ✳

The flavors of roasted ratatouille are intensified by herbes de Provence. If you have none on hand, use equal amounts of dried thyme, sage, marjoram, and rosemary.

SERVES 4

2 small zucchinis, cut into 8 slices lengthwise (about 1 pound)
2 red onions, thinly sliced
2 small red bell peppers, seeded and cut into 8 strips
Eight 1/4-inch slices eggplant, cut lengthwise (about 1 pound)
2 tablespoons herbes de Provence
1/2 cup balsamic vinegar
Freshly ground black pepper to taste
4 teaspoons olive oil
2 tablespoons finely minced Italian parsley
1/4 cup hot water
4 teaspoons finely minced garlic
4 teaspoons sugar
8 slices multigrain bread, lightly toasted
1 1/2 cups arugula, spinach, or watercress

1. Preheat the oven to 400°F. Spray a baking sheet with olive oil spray.

2. In a mixing bowl, toss the zucchini, onion, red bell pepper, eggplant, herbes de Provence, 6 tablespoons balsamic vinegar, and pepper. Toss to coat and spread on the baking sheet. Bake for about 30 minutes, tossing and spraying lightly again with oil spray after 15 minutes.

3. In a small bowl, whisk together the oil, parsley, water, garlic, sugar, and remaining vinegar. Spoon about a tablespoon of the dressing over each slice of toast, allowing it to soak in. Use all of the dressing.

4. Divide the mixed vegetables equally onto 4 slices of toast. Top each with arugula. Place the other slices on top, dressing side down, and serve immediately.

Cal. 270 Carb. 57g Prot. 9g Chol. 0mg Fat 6g/20% Sod. 239mg

> "*No one can persuade another to change. Each of us guards a gate of change that can only be opened from the inside.*"
>
> —MARVYN FERGUSES

* Red and Green Coleslaw *

These days, with preshredded cabbage, making coleslaw takes about thirty seconds.

SERVES 2

3 tablespoons apple cider vinegar
1 tablespoon plus 1 teaspoon sugar
3 tablespoons nonfat sour cream
1 1/3 cups shredded mixed green and red cabbage
Salt and freshly ground black pepper

In a mixing bowl, combine the vinegar, sugar, and sour cream and mix until smooth. Add the cabbage and toss to coat well. Season with salt and pepper. Refrigerate for at least 1 hour to allow the flavors to blend before serving.

Cal. 61   Carb. 15g   Prot. 2g   Chol. 0mg   Fat 0.13g/2%   Sod. 23mg

* Roasted Pepper Quesadillas *

Quesadillas are really very simple to make at home.

SERVES 4

2 tablespoons Nonfat Blend (see page 21)
1 tablespoon Spinach Pesto (see page 79)
1 tablespoon minced seeded jalapeño
$^1/_2$ teaspoon crushed red pepper flakes
Freshly ground black pepper to taste
2 large flour tortillas (about 10 inches)
$^1/_4$ cup minced scallions, green part only
$^1/_2$ cup minced red onion
$^1/_2$ cup each roasted, peeled, and diced red and yellow bell peppers (see page 31)
$^1/_2$ cup shredded Monterey Jack cheese
$^1/_2$ cup shredded white Cheddar cheese
1 tablespoon chopped fresh cilantro

1. Preheat the oven to 450°F.
2. In a small mixing bowl, combine the Nonfat Blend, Spinach Pesto, jalapeño, red pepper flakes, and black pepper and mix well.
3. Place the tortillas on a baking sheet sprayed with olive oil spray. Spread half the Nonfat Blend mixture on each, leaving a border.
4. Sprinkle the tortillas evenly with the scallions, onion, roasted peppers, and cheeses. Sprinkle the cilantro on 1 tortilla and place the other tortilla on top of it. Bake for 8 to 10 minutes, until the cheese melts. Slice into wedges and serve warm.

Cal. 228   Carb. 20g   Prot. 11g   Chol. 28mg   Fat 11g/45%   Sod. 173mg

* Roasted Vegetable Feast *

This beautiful array of roasted, grilled, and steamed vegetables is a true celebration of the garden's bounty. It's a vegetarian's dream, everyone's delight.

SERVES 4

1 pound small red potatoes
2 small eggplants, cut into eight ¹/₂-inch slices (about 1 pound)
2 small red onions, quartered
2 leeks, halved
4 plum tomatoes
2 large red bell peppers, roasted, peeled, and coarsely chopped
   (see page 31)
¹/₄ cup red wine vinegar
2 tablespoons finely minced garlic
¹/₂ cup coarsely chopped fresh parsley
Kosher salt and freshly ground black pepper
¹/₂ pound asparagus, trimmed
¹/₂ pound green beans, trimmed
¹/₂ pound sugar snap peas, trimmed
2 tablespoons finely minced chives
8 whole heads garlic, roasted (see page 66)

1. Preheat the oven to 400°F. Lightly spray a roasting pan with olive oil spray.
2. Spread the potatoes in the pan and roast for about 45 minutes, until tender and crispy.
3. Preheat the broiler. Place the eggplant, onions, and leeks in a roasting pan, keeping the vegetables separate. Spray with olive oil spray and broil 5 to 6 inches from the heat source for 3 to 4 minutes on each side, until golden. Set aside.
4. Cut the tomatoes in half horizontally and lay them on a baking sheet, cut side up. Broil for about 5 minutes, until they begin to brown.

5. Cut the eggplant into $1/2$-inch strips and the tomatoes into large chunks, removing the skin of both as you do so. Transfer the eggplant, tomatoes, onions, leeks, and potatoes to a bowl and toss with the pepper, vinegar, minced garlic, and 6 tablespoons chopped parsley. Season to taste with salt and pepper and set aside.

6. Put the asparagus and beans in a steaming basket set over 2 inches of boiling water and steam for 2 minutes. Add the peas and continue steaming for about 1 minute longer, until the vegetables are crisp-tender. Transfer to a bowl and spray with olive oil spray. Add the chives and toss well.

7. Arrange all the vegetables and the roasted garlic on a large platter or divide among 4 plates. Sprinkle lightly with the remaining chopped parsley and serve at room temperature.

Cal. 170   Carb. 37g   Prot. 7g   Chol. 0mg   Fat 2g/9%   Sod. 40mg

* Roasted Vegetable Mélange *

Too often, vegetables roasted in the oven are swimming in olive oil. Just 2 teaspoons enriches the flavor—no need for another drop.

SERVES 4

1 zucchini, halved lengthwise and cut into ³/₄-inch chunks
2 cups broccoli florets
1 leek, thinly sliced (about 8 ounces)
¹/₂ pound asparagus, trimmed, if necessary, and cut into 3-inch lengths
¹/₂ pound baby carrots, peeled and trimmed
12 shallots, peeled
20 cloves garlic
8 sprigs fresh thyme
2 teaspoons olive oil
1 cup low-fat, low-sodium chicken broth
¹/₂ pound cherry tomatoes
2 tablespoons finely minced fresh dill
¹/₄ cup finely minced fresh Italian parsley
Salt and freshly ground black pepper to taste

1. Preheat the oven to 350°F.
2. Arrange the zucchini, broccoli, leek, asparagus, and carrots in two 9 × 13-inch roasting pans. Divide the shallots, garlic, thyme, oil, and chicken broth between the pans and toss well.
3. Bake for 1¹/₂ hours, tossing every 15 minutes. Add the tomatoes and bake for 30 minutes longer. Season with the dill, parsley, and salt and pepper.

NOTE: This works well with quartered russet potatoes, frozen, thawed peas, and frozen, thawed artichoke hearts, too.

Cal. 171   Carb. 32g   Prot. 7.5g   Chol. 0mg   Fat 3.7g/18%   Sod. 199mg

* Roasted Whole Garlic *

Roasted whole heads of garlic are luscious. Squeeze the pulp from the skin and spread it on thick slices of toasted peasant bread.

MAKES 4 HEADS GARLIC

4 whole heads garlic
2 tablespoons olive oil
1½ cups low-fat, low-sodium chicken broth

1. Preheat the oven to 350°F.
2. Carefully remove the outer papery skin from the garlic heads, leaving the whole heads intact.
3. Arrange the garlic heads in a small baking dish so that they fit comfortably. Sprinkle with oil and add the chicken broth. Bake, basting frequently, for 1 to 1¼ hours. Cool slightly before serving or using in a recipe.

Cal. 79   Carb. 12g   Prot. 3g   Chol. 0mg   Fat 2.4g/25%   Sod. 216mg
(analyzed per head)

> *"There is no such thing as a little garlic."*
> —ARTHUR BAER

GARLIC

- The more finely you mince garlic, the more its oils are exposed to air, increasing its power and flavor.
- To tame the heat a bit, sauté with onions just until tender. Garlic becomes bitter when browned too much.
- If garlic has simmered in a dish and you want added punch, add minced fresh garlic at the end, too.
- Roasted garlic tastes nutty and sweet and loses its punch.
- Place whole heads in charcoal embers until the outside is charred and the inside is soft. Spread on grilled meat, vegetables, or bread.
- Choose large, plump, firm bulbs.
- Store in a cool place—but don't refrigerate.

* Sassy Salad Dressings *

Drowning wonderful fresh salad greens with a heavy oil-based or fatty dairy dressing is a common mistake. It can increase your fat intake faster than you can imagine.

Luckily, over the years, I've evolved to where I like my dressings to rely on flavors other than oil. Sometimes I use just a squeeze of lemon or lime juice to wake up the greens. Sometimes I want more intriguing flavors.

All of these dressings have big, intense flavors, so just a tablespoon sprayed or splashed on a cup of greens is delicious. Some of the fat percentages may look high. But check the grams; they're quite low. And remember, you're tossing the dressing over lots of good things.

TOMATO-BASIL DRESSING

MAKES ABOUT ²/₃ CUP

²/₃ cup buttermilk
2 teaspoons tomato paste
1 tablespoon finely minced fresh basil
2 teaspoons finely minced garlic
Freshly ground black pepper to taste
1 large plum tomato, finely chopped
Salt to taste (optional)

In a blender, blend the buttermilk, tomato paste, basil, garlic, and pepper until smooth. Stir in the tomatoes. Season with salt, if desired. Transfer to a jar with a tight-fitting lid and refrigerate until ready to use. Whisk before using.

Cal. 9   Carb. 1g   Prot. 0.6g   Chol. 0.5mg   Fat 0.2g/16%   Sod. 24mg
(analyzed per tablespoon)

BUTTERMILK

Buttermilk contains no butter. Originally a by-product of butter making, authentic buttermilk is almost impossible to buy today.

Commercial cultured buttermilk is milk that is artificially soured. Its lower fat content gives it a longer shelf life. It's great for baking, in dips, and in salad dressings.

In recipes with baking powder, you can substitute buttermilk for whole sweet milk. For each cup of buttermilk, reduce the recipe's baking powder by 2 teaspoons and add $1/2$ teaspoon baking soda. This ensures the proper proportion of acid and alkali needed for leavening.

WATERCRESS DRESSING

MAKES ABOUT $1/2$ CUP

1 cup watercress
2 scallions, coarsely chopped
1 tablespoon white wine vinegar
2 tablespoons low-fat, low-sodium chicken broth
1 teaspoon lemon juice
1 teaspoon finely minced lemon zest
1 tablespoon hot water
Salt and freshly ground black pepper to taste (optional)

In a blender, blend the ingredients until smooth. Season with salt and pepper, if desired. Transfer to a jar with a tight-fitting lid and refrigerate until ready to use. Whisk before using.

Cal. 2.6   Carb. 0.5g   Prot. 0.2g   Chol. 0mg   Fat 0.01g/4%   Sod. 11mg
(analyzed per tablespoon)

MANGO CHUTNEY DRESSING

MAKES ABOUT 3/4 CUP

2/3 cup nonfat plain yogurt
2 tablespoons mango chutney
Salt and freshly ground black pepper to taste (optional)

In a blender, blend the ingredients until smooth. Season with salt and pepper, if desired. Transfer to a jar with a tight-fitting lid and refrigerate until ready to use. Whisk before using.

Cal. 9   Carb. 1g   Prot. 0.8g   Chol. 0.2mg   Fat 0.03g/3%   Sod. 10mg

(analyzed per tablespoon)

FETA DRESSING

MAKES ABOUT 3/4 CUP

2/3 cup buttermilk
1 teaspoon finely minced garlic
1 tablespoon lemon juice
1 teaspoon finely minced lemon zest
3 tablespoons crumbled feta cheese
Salt and freshly ground black pepper to taste (optional)

In a blender, blend the ingredients until smooth. Season with salt and pepper, if desired. Transfer to a jar with a tight-fitting lid and refrigerate until ready to use. Whisk before using.

Cal. 16   Carb. 1g   Prot. 1g   Chol. 3.9mg   Fat 0.9g/51%   Sod. 57mg

(analyzed per tablespoon)

COOL CUCUMBER DRESSING

MAKES ABOUT 1 CUP

2/3 cup nonfat plain yogurt
1/2 cup peeled and chopped cucumber
1 teaspoon finely minced garlic
1 teaspoon lemon juice
2 tablespoons finely minced fresh dill
Salt and freshly ground black pepper to taste (optional)

In a blender, blend the ingredients until smooth. Season with salt and pepper, if desired. Transfer to a jar with a tight-fitting lid and refrigerate until ready to use. Whisk before using.

Cal. 5.4   Carb. 0.7g   Prot. 0.4g   Chol. 0.2mg   Fat 0.01g/1%   Sod. 7mg
(analyzed per tablespoon)

TARRAGON-BUTTERMILK DRESSING

MAKES ABOUT 2/3 CUP

2/3 cup buttermilk
1 teaspoon grated onion
1 teaspoon finely minced garlic
1 teaspoon dried tarragon
Salt and freshly ground black pepper to taste (optional)

In a blender, blend the ingredients until smooth. Season with salt and pepper, if desired. Transfer to a jar with a tight-fitting lid and refrigerate until ready to use. Whisk before using.

Cal. 7   Carb. 0.9g   Prot. 0.6g   Chol. 0.5mg   Fat 0.14g/18%   Sod. 16mg
(analyzed per tablespoon)

WHITE WINE DRESSING

MAKES ABOUT 1/2 CUP

2 teaspoons finely minced orange zest
3 tablespoons orange juice
2 tablespoons white wine vinegar
2 teaspoons soy sauce
1/2 teaspoon Dijon mustard
2 teaspoons sesame oil
1 teaspoon brown sugar
Salt and freshly ground black pepper to taste (optional)

In a small bowl, combine the ingredients. Season with salt
and pepper, if desired. Cover and refrigerate until needed.
Whisk before using.

Cal. 17   Carb. 1.5g   Prot. 0.13g   Chol. 0mg   Fat 1.2g/62%   Sod. 93.4mg
(analyzed per tablespoon)

ORANGE-BASIL DRESSING

MAKES ABOUT 1/3 CUP

2 tablespoons orange juice
1/4 cup white wine vinegar
2 tablespoons finely minced fresh basil
1 teaspoon finely minced garlic
1 teaspoon finely minced orange zest
Salt and freshly ground black pepper to taste (optional)

In a blender, blend the ingredients until smooth. Season
with salt and pepper, if desired. Transfer to a jar with a
tight-fitting lid and refrigerate until ready to use. Whisk
before using.

Cal. 3.4   Carb. 0.7g   Prot. 0.05g   Chol. 0mg   Fat 0.01g/3%   Sod. 0.09mg
(analyzed per tablespoon)

SHERRY WINE VINEGAR DRESSING

MAKES ABOUT 1/3 CUP

2 tablespoons sherry wine vinegar
3 tablespoons hot water
2 teaspoons capers
1 tablespoon olive oil
Salt and freshly ground black pepper to taste (optional)

In a small bowl, combine the vinegar, water, and capers. Slowly drizzle in the olive oil, whisking continuously, to emulsify. Season with salt and pepper, if desired. Cover and refrigerate until ready to use. Whisk before using.

Cal. 16   Carb. 0.6g   Prot. 0.15g   Chol. 0mg   Fat 1.7g/84%   Sod. 75mg
(analyzed per tablespoon)

ORANGE DRESSING

MAKES 1 SCANT CUP

2/3 cup nonfat plain yogurt
1/4 cup orange juice
1 tablespoon lemon juice
1 teaspoon finely minced orange zest
1 teaspoon honey
Salt and freshly ground black pepper to taste (optional)

In a blender, blend the ingredients until smooth. Season with salt and pepper, if desired. Transfer to a jar with a tight-fitting lid and refrigerate until ready to use. Whisk before using.

Cal. 12   Carb. 2g   Prot. 0.8g   Chol. 0.2mg   Fat 0.04g/3%   Sod. 11mg
(analyzed per tablespoon)

ORANGE-BALSAMIC DRESSING

MAKES ABOUT 1 CUP

$1/2$ cup orange juice
$1/2$ cup balsamic vinegar
1 tablespoon finely minced garlic
$1/4$ teaspoon freshly ground black pepper
2 tablespoons sugar
1 tablespoon finely minced orange zest
Salt to taste (optional)

In a small bowl, combine the ingredients. Season with salt, if desired. Cover and refrigerate until ready to use. Whisk before using.

Cal. 12   Carb. 3g   Prot. 0g   Chol. 0mg   Fat 0g/0%   Sod. 0.4mg
(analyzed per tablespoon)

"*Almost every person has something secret he likes to eat.*"

—M.F.K. FISHER

* Savvy Spinach Salad *

This is as satisfying as ever because the spinach is still combined with the eggs, mushrooms, and now turkey ham for a slightly smoky flavor. Missing are bacon, egg yolks (cholesterol), and loads of oil (read fat). Give it a try—I think you'll be surprised at how fresh it tastes.

SERVES 2

4 cups cleaned, stemmed fresh spinach, torn into bite-size pieces
1 pound mushrooms, stemmed and quartered
$1/2$ cup fresh alfalfa or other sprouts
4 hard-boiled egg whites, coarsely chopped
8 scallions, green part only, coarsely chopped
1 ounce turkey ham, julienned (about $1/4$ cup)
2 tablespoons White Wine Dressing (see page 72)

In a large bowl, toss the spinach, mushrooms, sprouts, egg whites, scallions, and turkey ham. Chill for at least 1 hour before serving. Just before serving, add the dressing and toss to coat the leaves. Serve immediately.

Cal. 234   Carb. 34g   Prot. 30g   Chol. 7.6mg   Fat 3.9g/15%   Sod. 94mg

EAT YOUR SPINACH

Popeye's beat-'em-to-the-punch power source has become a modern-day magic bullet. Eat lots of this dark leafy green loaded with carotenoids and other nutrients to lower your risk of cancer and heart attack. Nobody's given us a magic number, but a cup a day can't hurt.

* Silver Dollar Corn Cakes *

During corn season, I frequently make these corn cakes for Sunday breakfast. I load the batter with more fresh corn than it seems it could possibly hold, and then add even more to heated maple syrup. These cook best when they're small.

SERVES 8

1¹/₂ cups pure maple syrup
2 cups fresh or frozen corn kernels
¹/₂ cup cornmeal
2 tablespoons all-purpose flour
¹/₂ teaspoon baking soda
¹/₄ teaspoon salt
1¹/₂ teaspoons canola oil
³/₄ cup buttermilk
1 large egg, lightly beaten

1. In a small saucepan, heat the maple syrup and 1 cup of the corn kernels over low heat for 10 to 15 minutes, until the corn is tender and the mixture is heated through.
2. In a bowl, combine the cornmeal, flour, baking soda, and salt. Stir in the oil, buttermilk, and egg until just combined. Gently fold in the remaining 1 cup corn kernels.
3. Lightly spray a nonstick skillet with vegetable oil spray and heat over medium heat until a few drops of water, scattered on the pan, evaporate quickly. Drop 1 tablespoon of the batter for each cake into the skillet and cook for 1 minute per side, or until lightly golden. Spoon the warm maple syrup and corn over the cakes and serve.

Cal. 255   Carb. 57g   Prot. 3.7g   Chol. 27mg   Fat 2.4g/8%   Sod. 189mg

✳ Simple Black Bean Salsa ✳

This quick and simple salsa is absolutely addictive. I make it all the time—and even if I'm out of cooked beans, I'd rather make it with canned than not at all. Serve it with chips, fajitas, or tortillas.

MAKES ABOUT 2 CUPS

2 cups cooked or canned drained black beans
¹/₄ cup finely minced fresh cilantro
1 tablespoon finely minced garlic
1 tablespoon seeded and finely minced jalapeño
1 tablespoon low-fat, low-sodium chicken broth

In a large bowl, combine the ingredients and stir with a fork, slightly mashing the beans. Serve immediately or cover and refrigerate until needed.

Cal. 10   Carb. 2g   Prot. 0.8g   Chol. 0mg   Fat 0.05g/4%   Sod. 115mg

(analyzed per tablespoon)

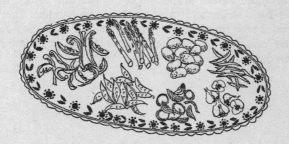

TORTILLA CHIPS

These are so easy to make and so much better when they are
your own and served warm from the oven with salsa or your
favorite dip.

MAKES 24 CHIPS

4 large flour tortillas (about 10 inches), each cut into 6 wedges

1. Preheat the oven to 275°F.
2. Lay the tortilla wedges on 2 baking sheets and bake for
about 20 minutes, turning every 5 minutes. Cool on wire
racks.

Cal. 18   Carb. 4g   Prot. 0.5g   Chol. 0mg   Fat 0g/0%   Sod. 56mg
(analyzed per chip)

SUGAR SNAP PEAS

These crispy, sugar-sweet peas eaten pod and all are by far
my favorites. A cross between an English pea and a snow
pea, they're also a "snap" to cook.

Every spring, when they're heaped high at the farmers
market, I try to include them in almost everything—soups;
the crudité basket; steamed in salads, rice, and pasta dishes;
stir-fries, stews, and unadorned by the handful. They're
loaded with protein and fiber, are fat- and cholesterol-free,
and have only 117 calories per cup. Steam or microwave.
But don't overcook or they'll lose their snap!

* Spinach Pesto *

After summer is over, large quantities of basil can be hard to find, not to mention very expensive. This convenient alternative to the classic basil pesto brings the same great flavors together and can be used just as you would the original Genovese favorite.

MAKES 2$^1/_2$ CUPS

16 cups fresh spinach, washed and stemmed (two 10-ounce packages)
$^1/_2$ cup low-fat, low-sodium chicken broth
1 cup grated Parmesan cheese
2 tablespoons minced garlic
1$^1/_2$ cups fresh basil, washed and stemmed
2 tablespoons extra-virgin olive oil

1. In a food processor fitted with a metal blade, purée the spinach a little at a time, alternating with the chicken broth until all has been added and mixture is smooth.
2. Add the cheese, garlic, basil, and oil and blend until smooth. Cover and refrigerate for up to 2 weeks.

NOTE: Parmesan cheese should always be aged Parmigiano-Reggiano—it promises the very best flavor for every gram of fat!

Cal. 24   Carb. 1.1g   Prot. 1.8g   Chol. 2mg   Fat 1.5g/54%   Sod. 71mg
(analyzed per tablespoon)

* Summertime Bruschetta *

Summertime tomatoes with their wonderful juiciness are the best for topping grilled crusty peasant bread or sourdough baguettes.

MAKES 8 SLICES

4 ripe plum tomatoes, very finely diced
1 tablespoon finely minced garlic
1/4 cup coarsely chopped fresh basil
2 tablespoons finely chopped Italian parsley
2 teaspoons lemon juice
Pinch of crushed red pepper flakes
Salt and freshly ground black pepper to taste
Eight 1/4-inch-thick slices French or Italian bread
2 cloves garlic, halved

1. In a large mixing bowl, combine the tomato, minced garlic, basil, parsley, lemon juice, red pepper flakes, and salt and pepper. Toss well and set aside for at least 3 hours.
2. Just before serving, grill or toast the bread and rub one side with garlic. Place a dollop of the tomato mixture on top of each slice.

Cal. 141   Carb. 27g   Prot. 5g   Chol. 0mg   Fat 1.3g/8%   Sod. 274mg
(analyzed per slice)

* Sunny Greek Salad *

This classic is always satisfying, even when made with far less olive oil than usual. The smidgen of feta is important, because this wouldn't be a Greek salad without it. Don't worry that the warm water will wilt the greens—it won't.

SERVES 4

8 cups mixed greens, such as Boston, Bibb, or leaf lettuce
2 tablespoons lemon juice
1/4 cup very warm water
2 tablespoons finely minced fresh oregano
2 small cucumbers, peeled and thinly sliced (about 40 slices)
2 large plum tomatoes, coarsely chopped
8 scallions, green part only, coarsely chopped (about 1/2 cup)
1/4 cup capers
1/2 cup finely minced fresh Italian parsley
1/2 cup crumbled feta cheese
8 kalamata olives

1. Place the mixed greens in a large mixing bowl. In a smaller bowl, combine the lemon juice, warm water, and oregano and whisk well. Drizzle over the greens and toss thoroughly.
2. Divide the greens among 4 plates. Top each with cucumbers, tomatoes, scallions, capers, and parsley. Toss gently. Sprinkle the feta evenly over the salads and garnish each with 2 olives.

Cal. 99   Carb. 13g   Prot. 5.2g   Chol. 12.6mg   Fat 3.8g/35%   Sod. 180mg

SWEETER SWEET POTATOES

A sweet potato needs no adornment. Just pierce with a fork several times and bake at 400°F for 1¹/₄ to 1¹/₂ hours, until tender. When the potato is fork-tender, bake it for 15 minutes longer so the sugar caramelizes.

Longer baking will only make it sweeter. The portion nearest the skin nearly caramelizes, rendering butter or any added sweetness irrelevant. Just split open and enjoy. Served cold, it's a great sweet movable feast.

* Tomato and Arugula Salad *

I've not tired of this salad since I discovered it at Romeo Salta's in New York City in the late '60s. Romeo brought arugula from Italy for only three weeks each spring, and I was there as often as possible to savor it. Nowadays, it's easy to find arugula everywhere and very easy to grow yourself. And if someone else washes the sand from the arugula, I could eat this every day!

SERVES 2

2 cups arugula, washed and torn into bite-size pieces
2 plum tomatoes, quartered lengthwise
2 thin red onion slices, separated into rings
1 tablespoon Our House Dressing (see page 55)
1 ounce part-skim mozzarella, fresh buffalo mozzarella, or smoked mozzarella, sliced into 2 rounds

In a large mixing bowl, toss the arugula, tomatoes, and onion rings with the dressing. Divide between 2 small plates. Place a slice of mozzarella beside the salad and serve immediately.

Cal. 39   Carb. 7g   Prot. 2.1g   Chol. 0mg   Fat 0.9g/35%   Sod. 48mg
(with part-skim mozzarella)
Cal. 80   Carb. 7g   Prot. 5g   Chol. 11mg   Fat 4g/43%   Sod. 103mg
(with whole-milk mozzarella)

* Tuscan Potatoes *

This recipe is a classic that is usually tossed with loads of olive oil, which is truly unnecessary; a light coating will do.

SERVES 2

1 pound small red new potatoes
1 tablespoon finely minced garlic
1 teaspoon olive oil
1/4 cup minced stemmed fresh mint
Kosher or sea salt and freshly ground black pepper to taste

1. Preheat the oven to 350°F.
2. Scrub the potatoes, place in a shallow roasting pan, and roast for 1 hour. While still hot, halve or quarter any that are not bite-size.
3. Immediately transfer the hot potatoes to a medium bowl. Toss with the garlic, oil, mint, and salt and pepper. Taste and adjust the seasonings. Serve immediately or at room temperature.

Cal. 201   Carb. 42g   Prot. 4g   Chol. 0mg   Fat 2.5g/11%   Sod. 13mg

* Zucchini and Onion Sauté *

The deep flavors in this Italian classic are always satisfying!

SERVES 2

4 medium zucchini, grated (about 4 cups)
1 onion, sliced into thin rings (about 1 cup)
2 tablespoons finely minced garlic
2 to 4 tablespoons finely minced fresh tarragon, or to taste
1/2 cup low-fat, low-sodium chicken broth
Salt and freshly ground black pepper to taste

In a nonstick skillet, combine the ingredients, except the salt and pepper, and cook over medium-high heat for 10 to 15 minutes, stirring occasionally, until the zucchini wilts and begins to brown. Season with salt and pepper. Serve immediately.

Cal. 112   Carb. 24g   Prot. 7g   Chol. 0mg   Fat 0.8g/5%   Sod. 14mg

FRESH START FOR FRUIT
by Julee Rosso

Learn the best ways to use nature's plentiful bounty of fruits in your daily diet. Inside you will find such delicious creations as:

- Oven Puff with Fresh Fruit
- Granny Smith Applesauce
- Peach Cake
- Passion Fruit–Papaya Frozen Yogurt
- Fruit Smoothies

And many more!

Get a fresh start on your health without sacrificing the joy of eating!
Choose your favorite food category or collect all six cookbooks today.

Published by Ivy Books.
Available in your local bookstore.

FRESH START
FOR GRAINS & PASTA
by Julee Rosso

Julee Rosso will teach you inventive ways to use all types of grains and pasta in your daily diet. Look for such delicious recipes as:

- Shrimp and Artichoke Pasta
- Spicy Tomato and Sausage Lasagna
- Red Pepper Risotto
- Roasted Garlic Pasta
- Pasta Primavera Verde

And many more!

FRESH START FOR MEAT & FISH
by Julee Rosso

Discover healthful and easy new ways to prepare your favorite meat and fish dishes. Recipes include:

- Italian Meatloaf
- Grilled Veal Chops with Roasted Garlic Purée
- Best Ever Barbecued Ribs
- Rosy Shrimp Salad
- Peppered Tuna

And many more!

FRESH START FOR POULTRY
by Julee Rosso

Let Julee Rosso show you how to create healthy and delicious new poultry dishes. Inside you will find such tasty creations as:

- One Thousand Spice Chicken
- Everyday Garlic Chicken
- Turkey Paillard Piccata
- Lime Chicken Fajitas
- Turkey-Pesto Grilled Cheese

Any many more!

FRESH START FOR SOUP
by Julee Rosso

You will never think of soup in the same way after sampling the soups Julee Rosso has to offer you. Try your hand at:

- Forty-Carat Carrot Soup
- Pure and Simple Onion Soup
- Quick Black Bean Soup
- Chicken and Spinach Soup
- Rosy Tomato Soup

And many more!